D1197074

CENSORED ON THE JOB

YOUR
RELIGIOUS
RIGHTS

FAITH AND FREEDOM
SERIES

CENSORED ON THE JOB

YOUR RELIGIOUS RIGHTS

JOHN W. WHITEHEAD

MOODY PRESS
CHICAGO

All Scripture quotations, unless indicated,
are from *The Holy Bible: New International
Version*®. NIV®. Copyright © 1973, 1978,
1984, International Bible Society. Used by
permission of Zondervan Bible Publishers.
All rights reserved.

ISBN: 0-8024-6681-8

1 3 5 7 9 10 8 6 4 2

Printed in the United States of America

The writer of Ecclesiastes tells us:

Then I realized that it is good and proper for a man . . . to find satisfaction in his toilsome labor under the sun during the few days of life God has given him—for this is his lot. Moreover, when God gives any man wealth and possessions, and enables him to enjoy them, to accept his lot and be happy in his work—this is a gift of God.[1]

Thus, most Christians believe that it is part of their Christian responsibilities to be happy in their work and to include their faith in their daily employment activities. That is part of what Jesus Christ terms being "salt" to the culture.[2]

Yet, as secularism, and secularists, increase their authority, the restrictions on religious freedom of Christians and other religious persons will grow accordingly, for many view evangelical Christians as a "threat to democracy."[3]

Restrictions on religion in the workplace will be among the most important for several reasons. First, workplaces are power centers where important governmental, educational, and social policies and laws are determined and implemented. Second, the ability to provide for one's family necessitates involvement in America's workplaces by nearly every family in America in one way or another. Third, as discussed earlier, work, and thus workplaces, are related to one's biblical duties as a Christian.

Historical Context

Concerns regarding faith in the workplace are relatively new. There are various reasons why this complex issue has arisen in contemporary America.

First, late eighteenth-century and early nineteenth-century America was *culturally different* from today's America. Early America was agrarian and Black slavery flourished.[4] There were no colonial "employers" such as those in contemporary America with their vast numbers of diverse employees and offices around the world. The family farms and businesses, apprenticeships, and various other forms of work relationships in early America did not include the concept of what modern Americans refer to as "rights" for workers.

Second, early America was *different politically.* There was no national bureaucracy; the preservation of a decentralized government was an important goal of colonial government.[5]

Third, colonial America was an era of *established state religions.*[6] Although the state-churches were of different sects, they shared the common heritage of Protestant Christianity.

Americans *no longer share a truly common religion*. The Civil War[7] and the increased immigration of the 1800s eroded the earlier dominance of the Protestant religion in American society.[8] The immigrants represented a wide variety of ethnic groups and many of them professed religious beliefs different than those that were prominent in America at the time.[9] At the same time, the rising presence and influence of American Judaism, Catholicism, and lesser-known religious sects, such as the Mormons, further diminished the Protestant role as the nation's religious yardstick.[10] Recent figures testify to the current religious diversity in America. For example, at least 239 officially recognized religious sects and 1,300 "unconventional" groups exist in America today.[11]

Finally, *the demographics of America's workforce are radically different* today from any other time in this country's history. According to "Workforce 2000," a relatively recent study supported by the United States Department of Labor, the ability of employers to compete effectively, both domestically and internationally, will depend primarily on their success in attracting and hiring skilled and productive employees in a market characterized by rapidly changing demographics.[12] This means, among other things, that achieving productive and efficient work environments will depend, more than ever, upon the ability of employers to find politically and socially acceptable common denominators for their employees while they are on the job.

Modern America, as Arthur Schlesinger has suggested, is ostensibly moving toward "an open society founded on tolerance of differences."[13] Indeed, the proliferation, especially since the early 1960s, of laws, government policies, and court decisions that preserve and protect the civil rights of those who are different is a reflection of America's desire, and need, for such toleration.

A Problem of Toleration

With the increasing national will for, or at least lip service to, toleration, however, the matter of religion in the workplace is increasingly an issue. This is largely because, unlike all the other classes of persons protected by civil rights laws in the United States, religious employees are often not deemed politically correct. The maturing sensitivities of the American people for the rights and differences of others too often do not include the rights of religious people. Contrary to many popular assumptions, the rights of religious persons are not mutually exclusive of the rights of other individuals or classes of people. Yet, many public school, government, and employer policies appear to be premised on the notion that somehow they are.

8

Religious persons are often viewed or treated as annoying, dogmatic, or, to those who are not actually or overtly hostile to religious persons, simply irrelevant. This is occurring for at least five reasons.

1. *The definition of a minority.* One definition of a minority is "part of a population differing from others in some characteristics and often subjected to differential treatment."[14]

In the United States, people who hold to, profess, and act upon a belief in the traditional Judeo-Christian religion or ethic are increasingly being excluded from society in general and thus discriminated against both in the workplace and the public arena.[15] America is sometimes referred to as a "Christian nation." To many, this means only that a majority of Americans are churchgoers who profess a belief in God.

However, some Christians (often labeled "fundamentalists") are not included within this general category, for they reject as theological error the mere superficial acknowledgment of God. These Christians take their religion seriously enough to face social penalties and, thereby, discrimination for their religious viewpoints. Employers, lawmakers, and the judiciary often fail to recognize this class as a true "minority."

2. *Ignorance.* Many religious persons, and often their employers, do not have an accurate understanding of the

rights of religious employees either inside or outside the workplace.

Although many corporate policies and personnel departments have a clear understanding of legal requirements contained in laws such as the Americans with Disabilities Act, the Age Discrimination in Employment Act, EEOC guidelines, labor laws, and OSHA requirements, apparently much less is known about religious discrimination and existing legal protections for the rights of religious persons.

3. *Nature of religious persons.* The erosion of the rights of religious employees sometimes involves the nature of religious persons themselves. Religious employees often tolerate discrimination against themselves, for example, in the form of so-called humor or other offensive behavior that would be wholly unacceptable if directed toward other individuals, classes, or minorities.

This view may be validated by recent statistics from the federal Equal Employment Opportunity Commission. In 1993, for example, the EEOC reports that it received 87,942 claims, of which 31,695 were based upon race and 23,919 were based upon sex discrimination. During the same period, only 1,449 claims of religious discrimination were filed, the only smaller number being 1,334 equal pay claims.[16]

In 1994, race claims decreased by .1 percent to 31,656, sex discrimination claims increased 8 percent to 25,860, and disability discrimination claims increased 23.5 percent to 18,859. During the same period, religious discrimination claims increased by 6.7 percent, but only to a level of 1,546 claims.[17]

These statistics do not indicate that there is little discrimination against religious persons in the contemporary American workplace. The many calls, letters, and legal cases, for example, handled by The Rutherford Institute about religious discrimination in employment attest otherwise.

Rather, the low number of EEOC claims based upon religious discrimination may reflect the fact that religious persons often believe that it is biblically wrong to challenge employers through complaints or legal action. Religious persons are taught to and wish to be loyal and productive employees and citizens. Moreover, Christians are often taught to expect abuse or rejection because of statements of Jesus Christ, such as "All men will hate you because of me."[18]

4. *Employer needs.* In order to be successful, most employers must maintain a working environment that maximizes productivity, effectiveness, creativity, and efficiency. This logically includes the reduction of conflict and its sources, along with efforts to maintain overall workplace fairness and compliance with legal requirements.

As a result, employers must often

select among competing or conflicting rights and interests. This often means that the employer's management and financial and legal perspectives will be formed to accommodate the interest or requirement that appears most compelling or that best serves the employer's interests.

Legal concepts such as "undue hardship" and "bona fide occupational qualification" recognize the needs of employers in the context of employee rights. Yet, religious employees also have rights, and employers must increase their awareness of them.

5. *Privatization of religion.* There is increasing social and cultural pressure for religion to be merely a "private" matter. Although most people will not challenge the right to *be* religious, increasing numbers of Americans appear to believe that religion should be *exercised* only in private. As Justice Antonin Scalia noted in his dissent from the U.S. Supreme Court's graduation prayer decision,

> [c]hurch and state would not be such a difficult subject if religion were, as the Court apparently thinks it to be, some purely personal avocation that can be indulged entirely in secret, *like pornography, in the privacy of one's room.*[19]

Justice Scalia's comments were based on the majority opinion of the *Lee v. Weisman*[20] Court, which included the statement by Justice Anthony Kennedy that "[t]he design of the Constitution is that preservation and transmission of religious belief and worship is a responsibility and a choice committed to the private sphere, which itself is promised freedom to pursue that mission."[21]

General Legal Concepts

There are a number of protections for the rights of religious employees. The *First Amendment to the U.S. Constitution*, which prevents Congress from making any law prohibiting the free exercise of religion, provides a key defense of religious freedom in the workplace.

The most comprehensive and, perhaps, familiar statutory federal legal protection for religious workplace rights is provided by *Title VII of the Civil rights Act of 1964* (commonly known as "Title VII").[22] Also, judicial constructions of Title VII are usually applied to other employment discrimination statutes.

The federal *Religious Freedom Restoration Act of 1993* (RFRA)[24] provides that the government may not "substantially burden" a person's exercise of religion even if the burden results from a rule of general applicability unless the government demonstrates that application of the burden to the person (1) is in furtherance of a compelling governmental interest and (2) is the least restrictive means of furthering that interest.[24]

Finally, *state constitutions and local rules and regulations* often provide important protections for the rights of religious employees.

This booklet will briefly overview Title VII and a few specific situations where the rights of religious employees are most often at issue.

No Religious Discrimination

Under Title VII, a covered employer must not discriminate against any individual because of race, color, religion, sex (which includes pregnancy and childbirth), or national origin.[25] The duty to accommodate the needs of religious employees was incorporated into Title VII in 1974.[26]

Who Must Comply

A "covered employer" is any "employer of 15 or more people in an industry affecting commerce."[27] The term "affecting commerce" is read broadly by the courts so that nearly any relation to interstate commerce means the employer will be covered by the Act.[28] Thus, most employers are subject to Title VII, including state and local government agencies that employ the specified number of employees.[29]

Religious organizations with the requisite number of employees are employers covered by Title VII. However, Title VII allows religions and religious educational institutions to discriminate in *hiring* on the basis of religion or religious belief and practices.[30] This exemption for religious discrimination by religious organizations is applicable to all activities of the religion, including secular enterprises. Thus, a religious organization may discriminate on the basis of religion in hiring and retaining employees, and the exemption does not violate the First Amendment's prohibition against the "establishment" of religion.[31]

The remaining restrictions against discrimination by religious organizations on the basis of race, sex, national origin, age, and disability are retained, but can, nevertheless, create tension between the statutes and the First Amendment prohibitions against infringing the free exercise of religion. Thus, the employer's activities (for example, the selection, dismissal, and discipline of ministers, priests, leaders, rabbis, or teachers) that go to the core of religious practices may not be challenged under these provisions.[32] Yet prohibited discrimination in a religion's secular activity or in the religion's treatment of support staff at religious institutions violates Title VII, and enforcement of the law does not violate the Constitution.[33]

Secular employers who are not "religious" but who wish to discriminate in favor of those with similar beliefs cannot claim the statutory exemption accorded religions.[34]

Definition of "Religion"

The Supreme Court has said: "Men may believe what they cannot prove.

15

They may not be put to the proof of their religious doctrines or beliefs. Religious experiences which are as real as life to some may be incomprehensible to others."[35] Even though they may consider some beliefs "incomprehensible" or "politically incorrect," employers and corporate personnel departments are not free to reject them. The role of employers is only to determine whether the beliefs are actually religious and if the beliefs are sincerely held—in accordance with the requirements of the law.[36]

As to the first inquiry, whether the belief is "religious," the United States Supreme Court has said that legally recognizable religious beliefs are those beliefs that are related to or parallel to a belief in a Supreme Being, involve duties beyond human relationships, and are not essentially political, sociological, or philosophical views, or a merely personal moral code.[37]

In order for the court to hold that a belief is sincerely held, the belief must be "based upon a power or being, or upon faith to which all else is ultimately dependent. A sincere and meaningful belief which occupies in the life of its possessor a place parallel to that filled by the God."[38] The Supreme Court has also said that courts must allow for "intrafaith differences."[39]

Title VII does not define "religion" except to provide that religion includes "all aspects of religious observance and practice, as well as belief."[40] Secular or social activities, such as church picnics, may not be "religious practices" even though sponsored by a religious organization.[41] However, protected religious practices do include the grooming and clothing requirements of one's religious faith.[42]

The practice does not have to be *required* by one's religion, but it will be included within Title VII's protection if the practice is performed *as part of* one's religious duties.[43] In *Frazee v. Illinois Department of Employment Security*,[44] a case handled by The Rutherford Institute, the Supreme Court dealt with this issue and said:

> [We] reject the notion that to claim the protection of the Free Exercise Clause, one must be responding to the commands of a particular religious organization.[45]

The EEOC has adopted a broad definition of "religious belief or practice." For the EEOC, "religion" includes faiths such as Latter-Day Saints, Black Muslim, Methodist, Baptist, Catholic, Judaism, Islam, as well as

> moral or ethical beliefs as to what is right and wrong which are sincerely held with the strength of traditional religious views. . . . The fact that no religious group espouses such beliefs or the fact that the religious group to which the individual professes to belong may not accept such belief will

not determine whether the belief is a religious belief of the employee or prospective employee.[46]

There is no requirement for a belief in a "god" as such, but "religion" or "religious belief" excludes mere personal preference grounded upon a nontheological basis, such as economic or social ideology.[47]

Nor are political beliefs or activities included within the definition of religion. For example, an employee's sincerely held views regarding military draft registration are protected as religion,[48] but Ku Klux Klan membership is unprotected political activity.[49]

Beliefs devoid of religious or moral content, regardless of how strongly believed, are not "religion" or "religious practice." Thus, one person's claim that eating cat food was a religious practice, because it contributed to the dieter's well-being, was not considered a "religious practice" because the practice did not relate to a "theory of man's nature or his place in the Universe."[50]

The fact that an employer does not agree with or even understand a particular religious view or practice is *legally irrelevant*, and employer actions based upon such disagreement or lack of understanding are actionable at law.[51]

Duties of Employees Claiming Religious Obligation or Practice

Employees seeking accommodation

of religious belief or practice have some obligations:

1. *Duty to cooperate.* Employees must cooperate with an employer or union in devising the accommodation, especially when such accommodations seem difficult.

In 1977, for example, a federal appellate court held that a bank was not obliged to accommodate the religious needs of a particular applicant for re-employment who sought a guarantee that she would never be called upon to work on a Saturday, which happened to be her Sabbath.[52] The applicant acted unreasonably by requiring the bank never to schedule her on a Saturday—a requirement the court found to be unreasonable and absolute in scope.[53] However, another case suggests that an employer must still make *some* effort at accommodation, even in the face of an absolute refusal to work on the Sabbath.[54]

2. *Duty to provide proper notice.* Employees are also obligated to give their employer *proper notice* of a religious belief or practice.

Employees who fail to provide such notice may waive any rights of accommodation normally available to religious employees. For example, giving an employer short notice of the need to take time off could defeat a claim of religious discrimination or failure to accommodate.

3. *Duty to make personal inquiry.* Religious employees should make a personal inquiry into their own motives and beliefs before seeking accommodation from their employers.

Religious employees must understand that mere distaste for a practice and a desire to avoid *all contact* with offensive ideas or practices of others in the workplace does not fall within the legal protection of Title VII.

4. *Duty not to unduly interfere.* Religious employees must try to avoid undue interference with the employer's operations.

When the practice of an employee's religious beliefs unduly interferes with the employer's operations, then the firing of that employee may not constitute a violation of Title VII.

For example, in a 1981 case,[55] an employee was terminated when he refused to follow the policies of his employers regarding a work environment found to be necessary to the employer's success.

The employee was a Black Muslim who believed that some of his managerial duties conflicted with his religious beliefs. He refused many duties, such as firing employees under his supervision and supervising certain activities. After a confrontation with his employers in which the employee refused to assume certain duties, he was fired.

The court found that the religious beliefs of the employee made him an ineffective manager and that his termination was justifiable.[56] According to the court, "Ali was terminated for a legitimate, nondiscriminatory reason sufficient to allow the trier of fact to rationally conclude that the employment action had not been motivated by discrimination."[57]

The Seventh Circuit Court of Appeals ruled in a similar fashion when an FBI agent refused to investigate certain groups charged with destroying government property as part of their expression of their opposition to violence.[58] As part of his Roman Catholic religious faith, the FBI agent found that he was unable to investigate a group of peace activists that included nuns and priests. When the FBI could find no one suitable to replace the agent on this job, the agent was told to take the assignment or face insubordination charges. The court found that transfers of work shifts posed an undue hardship for the FBI. Moreover, the

FBI treated the agent no more severely than it would have treated another agent who refused a direct order for secular reasons.[59]

Making a Case of Religious Discrimination Because of Religious Practice or Obligation

To prove a case of religious discrimination because of a religious practice or obligation, the employee must prove that the practice is "religious" and sincerely held, inform the employer of the conflict between the practice and the employee's job obligations, and be subjected to discriminatory treatment for complying with the practice.

Once the employee has met these requirements, the burden then shifts to the employer to show that accommodation was not required because such accommodation would have resulted in an undue hardship on the employer.[60]

Undue Hardship

The employer must then show "that he is unable to reasonably accommodate to [the] employee's religious observation or practice without undue hardship on the conduct of the employer's business."[61] "Undue hardship" excuses the employer from accommodating the needs of the religious employee. Undue hardship for an employer has been found where:

1. An employer would have to violate seniority provisions of a collective bargaining agreement;

2. An employer would suffer more than a *de minimis* loss of funds or efficiency to replace an absent employee; and,

3. Employees of other religions or nonreligious employees would be required to work at undesirable times to replace the absent employee.[62]

Unless undue hardship results, "all aspects of religious observance and practice, as well as belief" must be accommodated in a reasonable fashion by employers.[63] In this regard, an employer may not discriminate upon the basis of its speculation that an undue hardship *might occur* at some future time if an accommodation is made at the present time.[64]

Accommodation Standards

The federal EEOC has included accommodation standards into its Religious Discrimination guidelines.[65] The guidelines contain several alternatives that covered employers should consider as a reasonable accommodation for religious employees:

1. Employers should facilitate the securing of a voluntary substitute;

2. Employers should create flexible work schedules, such as flexible arrival and departure times, flexible work breaks, and use of lunchtime in exchange for early departure; and,

3. Employers should allow a possible job assignment change or lateral transfer so that time off for the religious practice would be available.[66]

Making a Case of Hiring and Promotion Religious Discrimination

In its 1973 decision in *McDonnell-Douglas Corp. v. Green*,[67] the U.S. Supreme Court established a four-pronged test for proving Title VII hiring and promotion discrimination. In this decision, the Court held that a complainant under Title VII must show:

1. That the complainant belongs to a class protected by the statutes;

2. That the complainant applied and was qualified for a job for which the employer was seeking applicants;

3. That, despite being qualified, the complainant was rejected; and

4. That, after rejection, the position remained open and the employer continued to seek applicants from persons of complainant's qualifications.[68]

Proof of these elements constitutes a *prima facie* case of religious discrimination in hiring and promotion prohibited by Title VII.[69] Once the complainant establishes a *prima facie* case, the employer-defendant must show, through the presentation of admissible evidence, a legitimate, nondiscriminatory, clear, and reasonably specific reason for its treatment of the complainant and that it actually used such reason in making its decision.[70] If the employer-defendant meets this burden, the complainant must then assume the burden of persuading the fact finder of the defendant's illegal motive. If the employer-defendant's action is motivated by religious discrimination, the action is illegal *even if all persons within the job classification are treated the same.*[71]

Specific Areas of Religious Discrimination

The following is a brief review of some of the areas in which religious discrimination claims most commonly arise and how the courts have generally decided the issues.

1. Discrimination Against an Employee Who Is Either of a Different Faith or no Religious Faith at All

Sometimes one's work environment becomes uncomfortable because of the religious or antireligious beliefs, practices, or values of the employer. Thus, an employer's implementation of religiously derived work rules or requirements, an employer's open discussion of religious faith in employment decisions, or the conduct of religious services or practices as part of the workplace environment or regimen may result in religious discrimination.[72]

An example of this situation is the case of an atheist bank teller.[73] In this 1975 case, an atheist employed as a bank teller in the defendant's bank refused to be present during the opening of monthly staff meetings once she learned that the convocation began with a short religious talk and a prayer, both delivered by a Baptist minister. The bank teller argued that such activities were offensive to her and that her compelled attendance constituted a violation of her rights under Title VII. Her supervisor refused to accommodate her concerns, telling her that if she did not like the prayer and discussion, she could simply "close [her] ears."[74] Her refusal eventually led to the loss of her employment at the bank.

The United States Fifth Circuit Court of Appeals found that the atheist bank teller had established a *prima facie* case that she had lost her job due to the discriminatory practices of her employer. In the words of the court: "The general rule is that if the employer deliberately makes an employee's working conditions so intolerable that the employee is forced into an involuntary resignation, then the employer has constructively discharged the employee and is liable as if it had formally discharged the aggrieved employee."[75]

It was irrelevant in this case whether the company intended to in any way proselytize the atheist. The fact that she was made to feel uncomfortable as a result of her employer's religious practices in an otherwise secular workplace was found to be enough to constitute religious discrimination under Title VII.

2. New Age and Other Employer Seminars

A frequently asked question involves compulsory attendance at employer seminars where material that is offensive to certain religious beliefs is presented. As mentioned above, federal civil rights acts require covered employers reasonably to accommodate the religious beliefs of their employees, unless such accommodation would create "undue hardship" on the conduct of the employer's business.[76] It does not generally create undue hardship for an employer to excuse religious employees from attendance at a religiously objectionable employer seminar. Federal regulations emphasize that "[a] refusal to accommodate is justified only when an employer . . . can demonstrate that an undue hardship would in fact result from each available alternative method of accommodation."[77] These regulations also provide that undue hardship usually exists only where accommodation of an employee's religious practice would create "more than a *de minimis* cost" to the employer or where the accommodation would require "variance from a *bona fide* seniority system."[78]

Excusing religious persons from attendance at, for example, New Age employment seminars, seminars on how to be politically correct, or seminars on sexual orientation matters that offend an employee's religious beliefs would not result in excessive cost to the employer or require the employer to interfere with the seniority rights of other employees. Indeed, it might be less expensive for the employer to have fewer employees attend such seminars and, with respect to seniority rights, it is difficult to conceive how excusing religious employees from attending a seminar could interfere with the seniority rights of other employees. This would appear to be possible only if excusal from employment seminars was itself one of the benefits of seniority, which seems unlikely.

Employers may contend that they have a *bona fide* interest in having all employees attend an employment seminar in order to improve the productivity and efficiency of their employees or to comply with legal requirements. If this is the case, objecting employees could be excused from that part of the employment seminar which is religiously objectionable. If the offended employees find the entire seminar to be objectionable, then the employer could meet individually with the employees to discuss neutral, nonobjectionable methods of improving employment productivity, efficiency, or compliance with legal requirements.

Again, the employer is under a *duty* reasonably to accommodate the religious beliefs of its employees unless the employer can meet the standards of the undue hardship test.

A decision of the Ninth Circuit Court of Appeals supports the idea that objecting employees should not be required to attend religiously objectionable seminars as part of their employment.[79] In this 1988 case, the employer was a manufacturing company owned and operated by two conservative Christians. The employer required all employees to attend a weekly devotional service, which included "prayer, thanksgiving to God, singing, testimony, and scripture reading, as well as discussion of business related matters."[80] An employee who was an atheist objected to attending the weekly services, but was told that attendance was mandatory. The employee filed a complaint with the EEOC, which filed suit against the employer in federal court.

The Ninth Circuit Court of Appeals held that the employer was not permitted to require the employee to attend the weekly devotional services.[81] Applying the federal statutes and regulations we have discussed, the court declared that excusing the employee from the devotional services was a reasonable accommodation of the employee's religious beliefs. The court also concluded that this accommodation would not result in undue hardship to the employer, notwithstanding the fact that some items of business were communicated to the employees at the weekly services.[82]

Just as the atheist employee in this case was excused from attending an employment meeting he found to be religiously objectionable, so also religious employees should be excused from attending employment seminars that they find to be religiously objectionable. This is true even if there are legitimate items of business discussed at the employment seminars. It is irrelevant whether the employer views the seminars as offensive or religious in nature. The law is concerned with the belief and practice of the religious employee.

3. Discrimination Between Religious Employees

Employers must sometimes select among competing demands, such as accommodation and business necessity. Sometimes the competing demands arise between the very groups the employer is attempting to accommodate.

In a 1983 case, a United States district court heard a police officer's claim of discrimination by the City of Chicago because members of certain "minority" religions were given additional holidays that he, a Protestant, did not receive.[83] According to the police officer, he received fewer paid holidays than members of other religions within the police force, such as Jews or Muslims, and therefore suffered an undue burden by receiving fewer paid holidays and being forced to work overtime and on otherwise undesirable assignments.[84]

The federal court found that even if there was no intent by the city to discriminate against the officer for being a Protestant, the fact that he bore an undue burden by being a Protestant at least provided the basis for his claim of religious discrimination.[85]

4. Religious Clothing and Personal Effects

Wearing religious clothing or keeping religious personal effects at the worksite sometimes gives rise to conflicts in the workplace. Cases have involved the yarmulke worn by orthodox Jewish men and the practice of married Muslim women of covering their entire bodies when in public except for their faces and hands.

At times, religious clothing or personal effects may interfere with the employer's duty to provide a safe working environment for the religious employee and others. However, the EEOC has established that unless some legitimate interest can be shown by the employer for the need to discriminate on the basis of religious clothing, such discrimination is unlawful.[86]

5. Grooming and Physical Appearance Determined by Religious Requirements

The personal physical appearance of an employee may not be regulated by a covered employer without a sufficient business justification.

In 1980, for example, a federal district court ruled that a company's no-beard policy could have a disparate impact on individuals who grow beards for religious reasons, and thereby put them in the unfair position of choosing between their religious dictates and their job.[87] In this case, the corporation had failed to prove the need for such a standard.

In another case, a court involved found that when certain physical characteristics, such as facial hair, threaten the well-being of an employer's business, then such a disparate impact could be deemed necessary and lawful. In this 1981 case, the EEOC brought an action against a Georgia restaurant alleging that it failed to accommodate a member of the Sikh religion who could not comply with the restaurant's facial hair standards as a result of religious beliefs.[88] As a Sikh, the employee was forbidden to cut or shave his facial hair, except for medical emergencies.[89] The man was recruited by Sambo's of Georgia to be a restaurant manager, but Sambo's had a grooming standard based upon its view that a significant segment of the market targeted and served by Sambo's preferred restaurants whose managers and employees were clean-shaven.[90] The manager candidate was, therefore, asked to shave his beard in order to receive his employment.

The federal district court held that such a requirement was a *bona fide* occupational qualification for a manager of a restaurant that relies on and appeals to the family trade.[91] The court ruled that the EEOC erred in holding that customer preference is not, as a matter of law, an insufficient justification for employer hiring requirements that may affect members of a certain religion.[92] According to the court, unless such discriminatory standards are shown not to have an impact on anyone other than the particular applicant, they could withstand scrutiny under the law and are proper where no possible accommodation exists that would rid Sambo's of an undue burden.[93]

Accommodation of religious beliefs regarding facial hair was also held to be an undue hardship where the job required wearing respirators, which could not be worn effectively by a person with a beard.[94]

Where the job requires a distinctive uniform for purposes of identification, such as airline employees or police officers, significant exceptions to the required uniform may impose an undue hardship on the employer and thus would generally supersede religious needs.[95] Nonetheless, some courts have held that police officers may use their uniforms as a means of religious expression in certain cases. These decisions have specifically approved the wearing of a cross or similar religious symbol, and the refusal to wear certain decorations for religious reasons.[96] However, *esprit de corps* or the desire to promote a corporate or other "image" may not be sufficient to require infringement of a religious employee's beliefs.[97]

6. Schedule Requirements

Many employment conflicts concern schedule requirements. Usually, an employer who is notified of a conflict between religious practice and a work schedule can find a way to accommodate the problem without undue hardship and is required to do so where this is true. The employer must take steps to adjust the schedule if possible and must also facilitate a voluntary adjustment of working times between employees (for example, by publicizing the religious employee's needs through a company newsletter or bulletin board).[98] An employer would be acting unreasonably if he or she arbitrarily denied the employee the right to use personal leave or vacation time for religious observances.[99] Reasonable accommodation of religious schedule needs also requires that the employer accept employee-arranged changes unless there is a legitimate reason not to do so. The employer, however, does not have to permit the employee to work overtime in order to make up any unpaid religious leave.[100]

A 1978 case[101] concerned an individual who was fired from his job when he failed to report to his job on a Saturday after informing his supervisor that he conducted Bible study classes on Saturdays. The employee claimed that, as a Sabbatarian, he was under a "religious obligation" to fulfill his lifetime appointment by his elders to be the leader of Bible study classes and had done so for many years prior to being fired. The employer emphasized the importance of having its employees work on necessary days and did not agree that the employee's religious beliefs absolutely required him to lead Bible study classes.[102]

The federal appellate court ruled, however, that the employee's participation in the Saturday Bible classes was well within the realm of a "religious obligation" protected by the law. It was up to his employer to prove that his absence on Saturday would constitute an undue hardship on its business. Since the employer had not made reasonable efforts to accommodate the employee's religious needs and had failed to demonstrate an undue hardship, the employee's religious needs were granted priority over the needs of his employer.[103]

7. Sabbath Requirements

Sabbath Day requirements present a more complex concern than do the occasional religious holiday or other intermittent religious schedule adjustments; thus, such requirements have resulted in numerous court cases.[104] This is because Sabbath accommodation requires a permanent adjustment of some fifty-two working days a year and an employee's paid leave time is not typically sufficient to cover such an adjustment. Even though the employer is obligated to see that this need for adjustment is communicated to other employees, in most situations other employees may not be willing to make adjustments that would result in their regular weekend work.

One adjustment that might be available is to allow the employee to make up his or her work on some other day if the work need not be performed on the Sabbath. Or the employee might not need to take off an entire day, so that the Friday concern could be met by simply leaving early so as to be home by sunset.[105]

Understaffing required by Sabbath accommodation has been held to be an undue hardship on the employer.[106] Also, distributing the work among other employees may be construed to be a discriminatory benefit *for* the employee seeking religious accommodation[107] and if distributing the accommodated employee's work among other employees imposes more than a *de minimis* burden on these other employees by making them work harder or for longer hours, the accommodation could constitute an undue hardship.[108] Thus, the employer must find a neutral way to accommodate the religious employee's requests while avoiding religious discrimination against the other employees.

If an employee is discharged for exercising Sabbath obligations imposed by sincerely held religious beliefs, the state may not deny unemployment benefits based on the exercise of this religious belief, irrespective of any or the lack of any Title VII claims against the employer. Such a denial would be an infringement of the First Amendment's Free Exercise Clause.[109]

These concepts are demonstrated in the 1979 federal case of *Brown v. General Motors Corporation*,[110] in which the plaintiff was an employee on General Motor's assembly line in Kansas City. The plaintiff became a member of the Worldwide Church of God and came to believe it necessary to follow the church's requirement of Sabbath observance from sunset Friday to sunset Saturday.[111] When a shift change occurred, the plaintiff was told that he had to work at a certain time on Saturday or face termination. The plaintiff was fired when he failed to show up for work on Saturday. General Motors argued that it could not make an accommodation in this case because it feared that if GM hired other members of this denomination, it might eventually suffer an undue hardship.[112]

According to the court, General Motors did not prove that accommodation of the plaintiff's needs would give rise to any immediate additional costs or burden.[113] Speculation about such costs or burden, the court held, "is clearly not sufficient to discharge GM's burden of proving undue hardship."[114]

In another case, the United States Supreme Court held that a company's seniority system did not have to accommodate an employee's Sabbath needs because of undue burden.[115] In this case, an employee in a twenty-four-hour department became a member of a church which held that the Sabbath must be observed from sunset on Friday to sunset on Saturday. The employee originally was accommodated by being transferred to an evening shift. Accommodation of this employee's needs, however, resulted in, first, a loss of efficiency, and second, additional costs when the employee had to be moved to another location. The Court held that this represented undue hardship on the employer.[116]

8. Abortion-Related Issues

The abortion crisis is increasingly resulting in workplace problems, ranging from simple expression issues to requests for reassignment and changes in duties. For example, in one case, an Internal Revenue Service employee who objected to processing requests for tax-exempt status for abortion clinics was assumed to be asserting a religious belief.[117]

In another case, a Florida court held in 1981 that an operating nurse who refused to perform abortions because of her religious beliefs was demoted wrongfully because of her refusal.[118] The court noted that the nurse could still assist in 84 percent of the procedures performed at the medical center and that the facility had done nothing to accommodate the nurse when she no longer could find other nurses who would switch schedules with her so that she would not have to perform abortions.[119]

Law enforcement officers have asked whether they must protect access to abortion clinics if they have sincerely held religious beliefs opposing abortion. Since the state's interest in this situation involves the public safety and enforcement of the law (however repugnant), the interest may be characterized as "compelling." Thus, a police department that fired or otherwise disciplined a police officer who refused to protect access to an abortion clinic would seem to be operating within permissible grounds, so long as the department treated the refusing officer the same as it would treat an officer who refused an order based upon secular grounds. Although a number of decisions have upheld police officers' rights to the free exercise of religion,[120] an officer's refusal to perform an assigned duty (a duty directly impacting upon public safety and the enforcement of the law) does not appear to be protected by Title VII, the First Amendment, or RFRA. The best course, then, appears to be to seek an accommodation or voluntary schedule adjustment with a fellow police officer.

9. Freedom to Espouse Religious Beliefs to Fellow Workers

Federal courts have held that when an employee espouses religious beliefs to others (including fellow employees or customers) to the point where such action interferes with normal business operations or violates a legitimate interest of employers, it is then proper for the employer to regulate such behavior.

For example, in 1986, a chaplain brought suit against his employers at a V.A. hospital when he was fired after the hospital claimed his evangelical approach interfered with his therapeutic duties.[121] The employer claimed that the chaplain exceeded the scope of his duty to lead recreational periods with patients when he had changed the format of the event to a Christian evangelical religious service in which he preached and encouraged participation in a manner that fellow chaplains interpreted as proselytizing.[122] The chaplain asserted that the central tenet of his beliefs (and the nature of his work as a minister) commanded him to act in whatever way possible to spread his beliefs and use the full potential of his pastoral experience.[123]

The United States Seventh Circuit Court of Appeals held that termination of the chaplain's employment did not violate the requirements of Title VII, or the Free Exercise or Establishment

Clauses of the First Amendment to the United States Constitution, which provide that "Congress shall make no law respecting an establishment of religion, or prohibit the free exercise thereof." According to the court, the fact that the discharged chaplain's conduct resulted in material and substantial interference with his therapeutic duties was sufficient to justify limiting his First Amendment rights to religious expression in a government institution.[124] The hospital had a legitimate interest in requiring its chaplain to perform as a "quiescent, passive listener and cautious counselor," rather than an active, evangelistic, charismatic preacher.[125]

Thus, when the practices of a religious employee, such as espousing religious beliefs in a certain manner, interfere with a legitimate interest of the employer's, that practice may be regulated without violating federal civil rights statutes. However, in the absence of such interference, employers may not regulate the expression of religious beliefs by their employees. As noted earlier, issues such as abortion and sexual orientation often give rise to attempts by employers to regulate workplace speech. It is important for employers to distinguish between legitimate employer interests and social agendas when formulating employer policies in these areas.

10. Religious Objections to Labor Unions

The federal government has sanctioned compulsory unions as part of its national labor policy and the National Labor Relations Act (NLRA).[126] Nonetheless, since 1980, accommodation of religious employees is required with respect to membership in a labor union.[127] If an employee's religious beliefs preclude union membership or financial support thereof, the NLRA mandates accommodation of that employee's beliefs. Such accommodation usually includes payment to a nonreligious charity by the objecting religious employee in an amount comparable to the union dues.

Employees have some responsibility for reaching an accommodation with the union or the employers in such cases. For example, in a 1979 case,[128] an employee refused to join the union of his employer, Rockwell Corporation, as a result of his religious beliefs.[129] He also refused, however, to pay an equivalent amount of his union dues to any local charity and he refused the accommodation offered by his employer and the union, i.e., that he make a charitable contribution to his own church. He was therefore discharged.

The United States Court of Appeals noted that when an employee proves he informed his employer that the payment of union dues is contrary to his religious beliefs, the burden shifts to the employer to prove that the employer made a good faith effort to accommodate those religious beliefs and that those efforts proved unsuccessful.[130] The employer in this case showed the required good faith and reasonable efforts to accommodate the objecting employee's religious beliefs. The employee's refusal of any accommodation proposal constituted undue hardship for both the employer and the employee's fellow employees who were members of the union.[131]

More recently, in a 1990 case,[132] an assistant professor of electrical engineering at the University of Detroit refused to join the union but authorized the union to deduct the agency fees from his paycheck. However, the professor withdrew his authorization for payroll deductions when he discovered that the National Education Association (NEA) and the Michigan Education Association (MEA), the organizations to which his dues were sent, had campaigned to protect a women's right to choose regarding abortion, a position that conflicted with his religious convictions.[133] The professor offered to pay an amount equal to the entire agency fee to charity or to remit that portion of his fee which was allocated solely to the union's local responsibilities and pay the balance to a charitable organization. The union rejected both offers, explaining that any accommodation must still include payment to the MEA or NEA, even if there was a reduction based on the abortion campaign issue. When he refused this, the university terminated the employment of the professor and he subsequently filed charges with the EEOC.

The appeals court found that Title VII entitles employees only to a reasonable accommodation of religious needs, not an absolute accommodation.[134] In this case, however, the court found that the union failed to make any reasonable effort to accommodate the professor's religious beliefs, which beliefs prevented him from associating in any way with the MEA and NEA.[135] The court ruled that the union was obligated to find some sort of reasonable accommodation, such as associating with the local professors' union, which had not taken a position on the issue of abortion.[136]

It should be noted that the federal Sixth Circuit Court of Appeals ruled in 1990 that the religious accommodation provision of the NLRA is unconstitutional under the Establishment Clause of the First Amendment.[137]

11. Religious Volunteer Work Is Not Protected Activity

An employee who chooses to take time off from work in order to do volunteer work for a particular religious

45

faith is not afforded accommodation protection unless such work is required at that particular time period by the tenets of the employee's faith.

In a 1982 case,[138] a Catholic employee of a Kroger Company meat packing plant volunteered to help make arrangements for a special Christmas Mass to be put on by local school children, including the employee's daughter.[139] The employee had volunteered to assist the children to get into their costumes and practice their lines one last time in order to perform the show that evening.[140] The employee believed it was her duty as a Catholic to do this in order to work at developing a close relationship with her daughter in a moral and religious environment.[141] She informed her supervisor of her need to take off on that particular day. Her supervisor, however, had already granted that day off to other employees and was unable to allow this employee the requested time off. Because she left anyway on that day, her employment was terminated. The employee filed religious discrimination charges, claiming that she was entitled to accommodation by her employer.

In this case, however, the court found that there was no requirement for Kroger to demonstrate that it could not have accommodated the employee's needs without undue hardship.[142] The particular activity was not mandated by her religious faith. Rather, it was a voluntary job that others could easily have done in her place. The court found that the employee had a duty to do everything on her part to help resolve conflicts between her job duties and her religious practices, and she failed in this duty when she made no attempt to reschedule the church function or to find a substitute.[143]

According to the court, the refusal to allow the plaintiff to leave early was not contrary to the plaintiff's religion and no person could have a *bona fide* belief that leaving in the morning to do tasks actually performed late in the afternoon would be contrary to religious belief or practice.[144]

Action Items

As discussed earlier, Christian employees have a religious obligation to *integrate their faith with their actions in the workplace.* As also discussed in this booklet, the U.S. Constitution and various laws protect the rights of religious employees to a degree. In order to continue to maintain the balance between religious beliefs and employer needs, Christian employees must take certain steps. A few of those follow.

First, religious employees must ensure that they, their employers, and their fellow employees *are no longer ignorant of the rights of religious persons.* Religious employees must ensure that infringement of their rights does not become the path of least resistance for their employers in achieving corporate goals.

To a large degree, this can be accomplished by a commitment to education and information. The civil rights of other groups have become respected and protected largely because such other groups have dedicated themselves to educating and raising the sensitivities of others about their rights.

At the same time, religious persons must be clear about distinctions between *essential rights that should be recognized* by their employers and *rights that might best be exercised outside the workplace.* This means that religious as well as nonreligious employees and employers must become knowledgeable about and respect their respective rights.

For example, an employee in a company has encountered difficulties in the distribution of literature by employees. This employee's employer provides a recreation/lunchroom where employees eat lunch and spend their break time. All these employees have traditionally enjoyed the privilege of sharing various publications and literature at that location until this employee brought a publication to work that a few other employees found offensive. Although a number of employees enjoyed the publication and requested copies of their own, others objected and the employer forbade the employee from bringing his literature to the lunchroom again.

The literature was not obscene or discriminatory—it was simply politically incorrect at that particular workplace. The employer's prohibition was based strictly upon the political incorrectness of the content—which represents the worst kind of employer response to situations like this. Publications that were personally offensive to the restrained employee were still permitted. Thus, this employer discriminated against this employee for his religious beliefs in its efforts to avoid mere offense to a few other employees who were simply more strident about their self-interest.

Second, religious persons *must insist upon a renewed understanding that the rights of religious employees are as important as the rights of any other individual or class or minority.* This is true not only from an ethical perspective, but also from the perspective of the law. The law does not establish a "priority" of rights for individuals or classes or minorities. The law elevates no individual or class or minority over any other. Prohibitions against discrimination based upon race, color, sex, or national origin apply *with equal force* to discrimination based upon religion. Yet, as a result of ignorance, popular misunderstanding, apathy, and political or social expediency, employers and others often prefer the rights of one such class or minority over others. This must stop.

Third, religious employees *must work toward a clearer understanding that recognition of the rights of employers, religious employees, and other employees does not have to be an "either-or" proposition.* The law provides that such recognition can—and should be—a "win-win" situation. For example, the law recognizes the concept of "undue hardship" for employers while recognizing the need for the accommodation of the rights of religious employees. Indeed, if both sides are truly objective, most religious beliefs and practices of employees may be accommodated without material harm to the employer's interests.

Fourth, religious employees, like all employees and, more broadly, all people, *must learn to distinguish toleration and understanding from compelled personal acceptance of diverse religious or worldviews.* America is no longer homogenous, and toleration and understanding are prerequisites for a just American society. Indeed, as may be seen in the so-called ethnic cleansing of the former Yugoslavia and the liberation conflicts proliferating in the former USSR, the lack of such toleration and understanding can result in horrors that most people have, until recently, believed unlikely in today's world.

However, compelled personal acceptance of the beliefs of others is antithetical to fundamental human values and the very foundations of America. Thus, employers can and should promote toleration, but employers may not and should not compel their employees to accept as valid the views and lifestyles they must tolerate in the workplace.

Finally, religious persons *must resist the privatization of religion in the United States.* Religious persons must resist the view that religious beliefs may only be professed in private. Religious persons should campaign for and elect representatives to government who respect and protect the right of individuals, in contrast with the state itself, to be religious in public.

Religious persons must ensure that government authorities, the legal system, and their friends, families, and peers understand the difference between religious beliefs and practices established and exercised by the government and the religious beliefs and practices of individuals.

Conclusion

It is clear that Americans face and will continue to face many workplace challenges. One of these challenges is to protect rights and preserve unity while respecting and nurturing diversity. An equally significant challenge is to meet the biblical challenge to integrate our faith with our work.

Notes

1. Ecclesiastes 5:18–19.

2. *See generally,* John Whitehead, *Religious Apartheid: The Separation of Religion from American Public Life* (Chicago: Moody, 1994).

3. *Ibid.,* 21.

4. *See generally,* John C. Miller, *The Wolf by the Ears: Thomas Jefferson and Slavery* (New York: Free, 1977); Dumas Malone, *Jefferson and His Time;* Fawn M. Brodie, *Thomas Jefferson: An Intimate History* (New York: Norton, 1974); Richard B. Morris, *Seven Who Shaped Our Destiny* (New York: Harper & Row, 1973).

5. *See* Forrest McDonald, *E Pluribus Unum: The Formation of the American Republic,* 7th ed. (Boston: Houghton Mifflin, 1965); Samuel E. Morison and Henry S. Commager, *Growth of the American Republic* (New York: Oxford Univ. Press, 1980), 184.

6. *See* Leo Pfeffer, *God, Caesar and the Constitution* (Boston: Beacon, 1975).

7. *See* Winthrop S. Hudson, *Religion in America,* 4th ed. (New York: Macmillan, 1987).

8. *See* Donald L. Drakeman, *Church-State Constitutional Issues* (New York: Greenwood, 1991).

9. Hudson, *Religion in America,* 224.

10. *See* Thomas T. Handy, *Undermined Establishment: Church-State Relations in America, 1880–1920* (Princeton, N.J.: Princeton Univ. Press, 1991).

11. Henry J. Abraham, "Religion, the Constitution, the Court and Society: Some Contemporary Reflections on Mandates, Words, Human Beings, and the Art of the Possible," in *How Does the Constitution Protect Religious Freedom?,* Robert A. Goldwine and Art Kaufman, eds., (Wash., D.C.: American Enterprise Institute for Public Policy Research, 1987), 16–17.

12. Brookhiser, "We Can All Share American Culture."

13. It is important to distinguish "toleration of differences" from "multiculturalism." Toleration is simply respect for others, while many view a goal of the multiculturalist movement as enforcement of a value of equality upon all cultures, all ideas, and all religions.

14. *Webster's New Collegiate Dictionary* (1975), *s.v.* "minority."

15. *See generally*, Whitehead, *Religious Apartheid*.

16. U.S. EEOC statement, "EEOC Chairman Announces Task Forces to Address Operational Issues; Releases FY 1994 Enforcement Results," 1 December 1994.

17. *Ibid.*

18. Matthew 10:22.

19. *Lee v. Weisman*, 112 S. Ct. 2649, 2685 (1992) (Scalia, J., dissenting) (italics added).

20. *Id.*

21. *Id.* at 2656.

22. 42 U.S.C.A. Sec. 2000e-1–2000e-17 (1981).

23. 42 U.S.C.A. Sec. 2000bb.

24. The stated purpose of this legislation is to "restore the compelling interest test as set forth in *Sherbert v. Verner*, 374 U.S. 398 (1963) and *Wisconsin v. Yoder*, 406 U.S. 205 (1972) and to guarantee its application in all cases where free exercise of religion is substantially burdened." Pub. L. 103–41, 107 Stat. 1488 (1993).

25. 42 U.S.C.A. Sec. 2000e-2(a)(1).

26. According to the amendment, "The term 'religion' includes all aspects of religious observance and practice, as well as belief, unless an employer demonstrates that he is unable to reasonably accommodate to an employee's or prospective employee's religious observance or practice without

undue hardship on the conduct of the employer's business.'' 42 U.S.C. Sec. 2000e(j).

27. *Id.* Sec. 2000e(b).

28. *See Heart of Atlanta Motel v. United States,* 379 U.S. 241, 258 (1964).

29. *EEOC v. Monclova Township,* 920 F.2d 360 (6th Cir. 1990). The term *employee* does not include persons elected to public office and those personal staff members who work in policy-making positions. Such high-level policy makers are not counted for the purpose of determining the coverage of the governmental office. The 1991 Civil Rights Act specifically protects these employees against discrimination. *See Teneyuca v. Bexar County,* 767 F.2d 148 (5th Cir. 1985).

30. 42 U.S.C.A. Sec. 2000e-1 and e-2(d)(2).

31. *Corporation of Presiding Bishop of Church of Jesus Christ of Latter-Day Saints v. Amos,* 483 U.S. 327 (1987).

32. *Scharon v. St. Luke's Episcopal Presbyterian Hospitals,* 929 F.2d 360 (8th Cir. 1991).

33. *EEOC v. Southwestern Baptist Theological Seminary,* 651 F.2d 277 (5th Cir. 1981), *cert. denied,* 456 U.S. 908 (1982).

34. *EEOC v. Townley Engineering & Mfg. Co.,* 859 F.2d 610 (9th Cir.), *cert. denied,* 489 U.S. 1077 (1988).

35. *United States v. Ballard,* 322 U.S. 78, 86 (1944).

36. *United States v. Seeger,* 380 U.S. 163, 165–66 (1965).

37. *Id.*

38. *Id.*

39. *Thomas v. Review Bd.,* 450 U.S. 707, 715–16 (1981).

40. 42 U.S.C.A. Sec. 2000e-(j).

41. *Wessling v. Kroger Co.,* 554 F. Supp. 548 (D.C. Mich. 1982).

42. *Bhatia v. Chevron U.S.A., Inc.*, 734 F.2d 1382 (9th Cir. 1984).

43. *Redmond v. GAF Corp.*, 574 F.2d 897 (7th Cir. 1978).

44. 109 S. Ct. 1514 (1989).

45. *Id.* at 1517.

46. 29 C.F.R. Sec. 1605.1.

47. *Edwards v. School Bd. of City of Norton, Va.*, 483 F. Supp. 620, 624 (W.D. Va. 1980), *judgment remanded and vacated in part*, 658 F.2d 951 (4th Cir. 1981). *See also Yott v. North American Rockwell Corp.*, 501 F.2d 398 (9th Cir. 1974), *cert. denied*, 445 U.S. 928 (1980).

48. *American Postal Workers Union, San Francisco Local v. Postmaster General*, 781 F.2d 772 (9th Cir. 1986).

49. *Bellamy v. Mason's Stores, Inc.*, 368 F. Supp. 1025 (D.C. Va. 1973), *aff'd* 508 F.2d 504 (4th Cir. 1974).

50. *Brown v. Pena*, 441 F. Supp. 1382 (S.D. Fla. 1977), *aff'd mem.* 589 F.2d 1113 (5th Cir. 1979).

51. *See, e.g., Bellamy v. Mason's Stores Inc.*, 368 F. Supp. at 1026.

52. *Jordan v. North Carolina Nat'l Bank*, 565 F.2d 72, 76 (4th Cir. 1977).

53. *Id.*

54. *See E.E.O.C. v. Ithaca Industries*, 849 F.2d 116 (4th Cir. 1988).

55. *Ali v. Southeast Neighborhood House*, 519 F. Supp. 489 (D.D.C. 1981).

56. *Id.* at 495.

57. *Id.* at 497. The court writes:

> Ali's religious beliefs enveloped every facet of his life, personal or business. It must be evident that in SENH's employment no "reasonable accommodation," indeed, no accommodation at all, could make way for those religious beliefs as Ali envisioned them: "helping remake the world, changing ... people's minds and their relationship to

each other." Only a complete reversal of the employer-employee roles, with Ali in the former, rather than the latter, might provide the plaintiff the absolute power he requires to satisfy those beliefs. . . . Accommodation is not abdication. Title VII cannot and will not be so construed.

Id.

58. *Ryan v. United States Dept. of Justice*, 950 F.2d 458, 462 (7th Cir. 1991); *cert. denied*, 112 S. Ct. 2309 (1992).

59. *Id.* at 461. According to the court:

Sympathy for a dedicated agent trapped between his career and his faith comes easily. . . . It is difficult for any organization to accommodate employees who are choosy about assignments; for a parliamentary organization the tension is even greater. Conscientious objectors in the military seek discharge, which accommodates their beliefs and the military's need for obedience. Ryan received discharge but does not want it. He wants to be an agent and to choose his assignments too. With good will all around, and flexibility on the part of Ryan's fellow agents, it just might be possible to make a go of it. Title VII does not, however, compel the F.B.I. to attempt this. Legal institutions lack the sense of nuance that will tell an experienced agent how far the rules may be bent without injury to the F.B.I.'s mission. Compelled, as it is by Title VII, to have one rule for all of the diverse religious beliefs and practices in the Untied States, the F.B.I. may choose to be stingy with exceptions lest the demand for them overwhelm it.

Id. at 462. It should be noted that the Ryan court also said, quoting:

Employment Division v. Smith, 494 U.S. 872, (1990), that any argument that failure to accommodate Ryan's religiously motivated acts violates the free exercise clause of the first amendment is untenable. Smith holds that rules neutral with respect to religion satisfy that clause. The FBI did not hold Ryan's faith against him; it judged his deeds, not his beliefs, and treated him no more severely than it would have treated an agent who refused a direct order for secular reasons. Title VII requires of the FBI more than the Constitution in its own right. An employer may not discriminate on account of religion—that is to say, may not use an employee's religion as a ground of decision.

Section 701(j), 42 U.S.C. Sec. 2000e(j), provides that religion "includes all aspects of religious observance and practice . . . unless an employer demonstrates that he is unable to reasonably accommodate to an employee's . . . religious observance or practice without undue hardship on the conduct of the employer's business." *See generally Ansonia Board of Education v. Philbrook,* 479 U.S. 60, (1986); *Trans World Airlines, Inc. v. Hardison,* 432 U.S. 63, (1977). Religiously motivated selectivity in the work one is willing to perform is an "aspect of religious observance and practice" that the employer must disregard unless it demonstrates that it is "unable to reasonably accommodate . . . without undue hardship." *See Baz v. Walters,* 782 F.2d 701 (7th Cir. 1986).

Reallocation of work between agents is the most obvious accommodation, one that Ryan's fellow agents had arranged for him before. Because Ryan refused Swinford's offer to arrange for a swap this time, we need not decide whether a series of swaps—potentially calling for training a different agent in the techniques of domestic security investigations—would create "undue hardship" for the FBI as Hardison defines that term: "To require [the employer] to bear more than a de minimis cost . . . is an undue hardship." 432 U.S. at 84. *Accord, Ansonia,* 479 U.S. at 67.

Id. at 461.

60. *See Brown v. General Motors Corp.,* 601 F.2d 956, 960 (8th Cir., 1979). *See also* Ingram and Domph, *An Employer's Duty to Accommodate the Religious Beliefs and Practices of an Employee,* 87 DICKINSON L. REV. 21 (1982).

61. 42 U.S.C.A. Sec. 2000e-(j).

62. *Trans World Airlines, Inc. v. Hardison*, 432 U.S. at 85. *See generally* AM. JUR. 2d Sec. 63(B).

63. 42 U.S.C.A. Sec. 2000e(j) (Supp. II., 1976).

64. It is important to note that, after public hearings held in 1978, the EEOC reported that little evidence was submitted by employers which showed actual attempts to accommodate religious practices had resulted in unfavorable consequences to the employer's business. The EEOC report noted that while employers "appeared to have substantial anticipatory concerns," they had "no, or very little, actual experience with the problems" they feared would result from their reasonable accommodation of religious practices. 29 C.F.R. Sec. 1605.2, 1605.3, Appendix A (1991).

65. Section (c) of those guidelines states the following:

(1) After an employee or prospective employee notifies the employer or labor organization of his or her need for a religious accommodation, the employer or labor organization has an obligation to reasonably accommodate the individual's religious practice. A refusal to accommodate is justified only when an employer or labor organization can demonstrate that an undue hardship would in fact result from each available alternative method of accommodation. A mere assumption that many more people, with the same religious practices as the person being accommodated, may also need accommodation is not evidence of undue hardship.

(2) When there is more than one method of accommodation available that would not cause undue hardship, the Commission will determine whether the accommodation offered is reasonable by examining:

(i) The alternatives for accommodation considered by the employer or labor organization; and

(ii) The alternatives for accommodation, if any, actually offered to the individual requiring accommodation. Some alternatives for accommodating religious practices might disadvantage the individual with respect to his or her employment opportunities, such as compensation, terms, conditions, or privileges of employment. Therefore, when there is more than one means of accommodation which would not cause undue hardship, the employer or labor organization must offer the alternative which least disadvantages the individual with respect to his or her employment opportunities.

EEOC Religious Discrimination Guidelines, 29 C.F.R. 1605.2(c) (1991).

66. *Id.* Sec. 1605.2(d) (i–iii).

67. 411 U.S. 792 (1973).

68. *Id.* at 802.

69. *Id. See also Lawrence v. Mars, Inc.,* 955 F.2d 902, 906 (4th Cir. 1992), (plaintiff failed to present direct or indirect evidence of religious discrimination), *cert. denied,* 113 S. Ct. 76 (1993).

70. *Texas Dept. of Community Affairs v. Burdine,* 450 U.S. 248 (1981).

71. *See, for example, Gerdom v. Continental Airlines, Inc.,* 692 F.2d 602 (9th Cir. 1982)., *cert. denied,* 460 U.S. 1074 (1983).

72. Laura S. Underkuffler, *"Discrimination" on the Basis of Religion: An Examination of Attempted Value Neutrality in Employment,* 30 WILLIAM & MARY L. REV. 581 (1991).

73. *Young v. Southwestern Sav. and Loan Assoc.,* 509 F. 2d 140 (5th Cir. 1975).

74. *Id.* at 142.

75. *Id.* at 144.

76. 29 C.F.R. 1605.2(b)(1); see also 42 U.S.C. Sec. 2000e(j), 2000e-2(a)(1).

77. 29 C.F.R. Sec. 1605.2(c)(1) (italics added).

78. *Id.,* Sec. 1605.2(e)(1)–(2).

79. *E.E.O.C. v. Townley Eng'g. & Mfg. Co.*, 859 F.2d 610 (9th Cir.), *cert. denied*, 489 U.S. 1077 (1989).

80. *Id.* at 612.

81. *Id.* at 615–16.

82. *Id.*

83. *Ka Nam Kuan v. City of Chicago*, 563 F. Supp. 255 (N.D. Ill. 1983). *See also* cases listed at 563 F. Supp. 258.

84. *Id.* at 257.

85. The court did not rule that Mr. Kuan was discriminated against. Rather, they refused to dismiss the entire case and sent it back to the local trial court, in which the city of Chicago had fourteen days to answer Mr. Kuan's discrimination charges. *Id.* at 259.

86. For example, the EEOC ruled that a nurse who wore a head covering required by her "Old Catholic" tenet could not be discriminated against by a hospital who could show no legitimate interest for requiring the wearing of the traditional nurse's cap instead. EEOC Decision No. 71-779, 21 December 1970.

87. *Isaac v. Butler's Shoe Corp.*, 511 F. Supp. 108, 114 (N.D. Ga. 1980).

88. *E.E.O.C. v. Sambo's of Georgia, Inc.*, 530 F. Supp. 86 (N.D. Ga. 1981).

89. *Id.* at 88.

90. *Id.* at 89.

91. *Id.* at 91.

92. *Id.*, citing *Woods v. Safeway Stores, Inc.*, 420 F. Supp. 35, 43 (E.D. Va. 1976), *cert. denied*, 440 U.S. 930 (1979) (customer preference for overall store hygiene and an appearance of cleanliness in the retail food industry makes employee grooming standards that forbid facial hair a necessity).

93. *Id.* at 93.

94. *Bhatia v. Chevron U.S.A., Inc.*, 734 F.2d 1382 (9th Cir. 1984).

95. *Goldman v. Secretary of Defense*, 475 U.S. 503 (1986).

96. *Leonard v. City of Columbus*, 705 F. 2d 1299 (11th Cir. 1983), *cert. denied*, 468 U.S. 1204 (1984).

97. *Isaac v. Butler's Shoe Corp.*, 511 F. Supp. 108 (N.D. Ga. 1980). *Cf. Board of Educ.*, 911 F.2d 882 (banning public school teachers from wearing religious attire was valid in light of the public school's need to maintain religious neutrality).

98. E.E.O.C. Guidelines, 29 C.F.R. Sec. 1605.2(d).

99. *Ansonia Bd. of Educ. v. Philbrook*, 479 U.S. 60 (1986), *Brown v. General Motors Corp.*, 601 F.2d 956 (8th Cir. 1979).

100. *Getz v. Commonwealth of Penn. Dept. of Pub. Welfare*, 802 F.2d 72 (3d Cir. 1986).

101. *Redmond v. GAF Corp.*, 574 F.2d at 897.

102. *Id.* at 898.

103. *Id.* at 897.

104. *See, for example, Redmond v. GAF Corp.*, 574 F.2d 897 and cases cited at 900 n.8; and *Thornton v. Caldor, Inc.*, 472 U.S. 703 (1985); *Ansonia Bd. of Educ. v. Philbrook*, 479 U.S. 60.

105. *See Protos v. Volkswagen of America*, 797 F.2d 129 (3d Cir. 1986), *cert. denied*, 479 U.S. 972 (1986).

106. *Wisner v. Truck Center*, 784 F.2d 1571 (11th Cir. 1986).

107. This would be a form of religious discrimination prohibited under Section 703(a) of Title VII.

108. *Wisner v. Truck Center*, 784 F.2d 1571 (proof that no replacement hired does not prove plaintiff's services not needed on Saturday); *Mann v. Milgram Food Stores, Inc.*, 730 F.2d 1186 (8th Cir. 1984); *Howard v. Haverty Furniture Co.*,

615 F.2d 203 (5th Cir. 1980); *Johnson v. United States Postal Serv.*, 497 F.2d 128 (5th Cir. 1974).

109. *Hobbie v. Unemployment Commission,* 480 U.S. 136 (1987).

110. 601 F.2d 956 (1979).

111. *Id.* at 958.

112. *Id.* at 960.

113. *Id.* at 961.

114. *Id.*

115. *Trans World Airlines, Inc. v. Hardison,* 432 U.S. at 84.

116. *Id.; See also Cross v. Baular,* 477 F. Supp. 748, 753 (D. Or. (1979). See also *Edwards v. School Bd.*, 483 F. Supp. 620, 627 (W.D. Va. 1980), *modified on other grounds,* 658 F.2d 951 (4th Cir. 1981); *Yott v. North American Rockwell Corp.,* 602 F.2d 904, 907 (9th Cir. 1979), *cert. denied,* 445 U.S. 928 (1980); *McDaniel v. Essex Int'l., Inc.;* 571 F.2d 338, 343 (6th Cir. 1978); *Brown v. General Motors Corp.,* 601 F.2d 956; *Redmond v. GAF Corp.,* 574 F.2d 897.

117. *Haring v. Blumenthal,* 471 F. Supp. 1172 (D.D.C. 1979), *cert. denied,* 452 U.S. 939 (1981).

118. *Kenny v. Ambulatory Centre of Miami, Florida, Inc.,* 400 So. 2d 1262, 1267 (Fla. Ct. App. 1981).

119. *Id.* at 1266.

120. *See* Annotation, *First Amendment Protection for Law Enforcement Employees,* 109 A.L.R. Fed. 9, 226–27 (1992). A police officer may not be prohibited from reading the Bible during a lunch break or at other times when work would not be affected, *Roberts v. Madigan,* 921 F.2d 1047 (10th Cir. 1990), *cert. denied,* 112 S. Ct. 3025 (1992).

121. *Baz v. Walters,* 782 F.2d 701 (7th Cir. 1986)

122. *Id.* at 703.

123. *Id.* at 705.

124. *Id.* at 708.

125. *Id.* at 709.

126. National Labor Relations Act, 29 U.S.C. Sec. 169 (1981).

127. The relevant amendment to the National Labor Relations Act reads as follows:

> Any employee who is a member of and adheres to established and traditional tenets or teachings of a bona fide religion, body, or sect which has historically held conscientious objections to joining or financially supporting labor organizations shall not be required to join or financially support any labor organization as a condition of employment: except that such employee may be required in a contract between such employees' employer and a labor organization in lieu of periodic dues and initiation fees, to pay sums equal to such dues and initiation fees to a nonreligious, nonlabor organization charitable fund exempt from taxation . . . chosen by such employee from a list of at least three such funds, designated in such contract or if the contract fails to designate such funds, then to any such fund chosen by the employee. If such employee who holds conscientious objections pursuant to this section requests the labor organization to use the grievance-arbitration procedure on the employee's behalf, the labor organization is authorized to charge the employee for the reasonable cost of using such procedure.

National Labor Relations Act, 29 U.S.C. Sec. 169.

128. *Yott,* 602 F.2d at 904.

129. *Id.* at 906.

130. *Id.* at 907.

131. *Id.* at 908.

132. *E.E.O.C. v. Univ. of Detroit,* 904 F.2d 331 (6th Cir. 1990).

133. *Id.* at 332.

134. *Id.* at 334.

135. *Id.*

136. *Id.* at 335.

137. *Wilson v. N.L.R.B.*, 920 F.2d 1282, 1290 (6th Cir. 1990) *cert. denied*, 112 S. Ct. 3025 (1992).

138. *Wessling v. Kroger Co.*, 554 F. Supp. 548 (E.D. Mich. 1982).

139. *Id.* at 549–50.

140. *Id.* at 550.

141. *Id.*

142. *Id.* at 552.

143. *Id.*

144. *Id.* at 553.

Moody Press, a ministry of Moody Bible Institute, is designed for education, evangelization, and edification.
If we may assist you in knowing more about Christ and the Christian life, please write us without obligation: Moody Press, c/o MLM, Chicago, Illinois 60610.